A Kalmus Classic Edition

Ludwig van

BEETHOVEN

ECOSSAISES

Edited by Ferruccio Busoni

FOR PIANO

K 03190

Ecossaises

Ludwig van Beethoven
Arranged for concert performance
and dedicated to
Miss Gerda Sjöstrand by
Ferruccio B. Busoni

Leggero ed animato

Piano